Piano Solo

Disney
ENCANTO

Music from the Motion Picture Soundtrack
Original Songs by Lin-Manuel Miranda

ISBN 978-1-70516-709-0

HAL•LEONARD®

Visit Hal Leonard Online at
www.halleonard.com

World headquarters, contact:
Hal Leonard
7777 West Bluemound Road
Milwaukee, WI 53213
Email: info@halleonard.com

In Europe, contact:
Hal Leonard Europe Limited
42 Wigmore Street
Marylebone, London, W1U 2RY
Email: info@halleonardeurope.com

In Australia, contact:
Hal Leonard Australia Pty. Ltd.
4 Lentara Court
Cheltenham, Victoria, 3192 Australia
Email: info@halleonard.com.au

CONTENTS

ALL OF YOU

Music and Lyrics by
LIN-MANUEL MIRANDA

Moderately

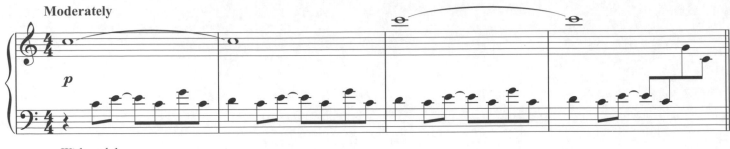

Pedal ad lib.

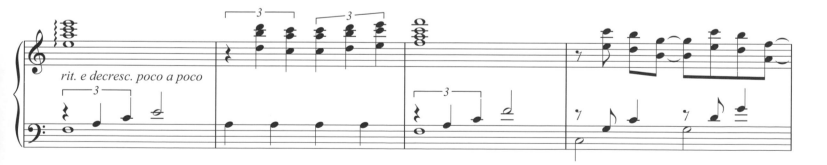

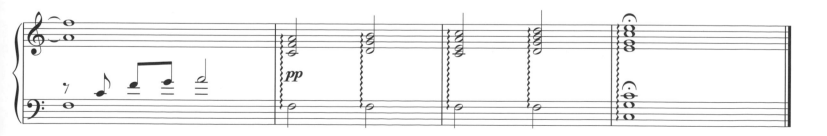

COLOMBIA, MI ENCANTO

Music and Lyrics by
LIN-MANUEL MIRANDA

Moderately fast

SURFACE PRESSURE

Music and Lyrics by
LIN-MANUEL MIRANDA

Moderately

Swing 16ths

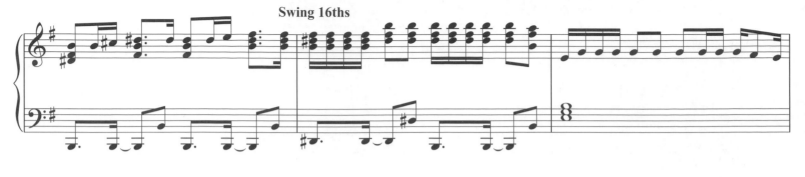

Straight 16ths

Swing 16ths

Straight 16ths

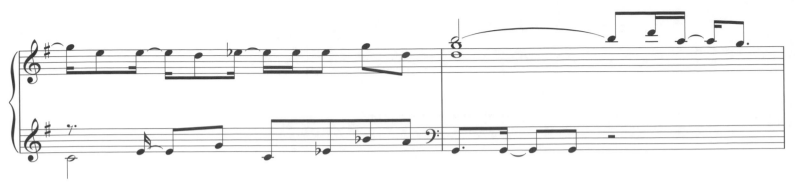

Swing 16ths

DOS ORUGUITAS

Music and Lyrics by
LIN-MANUEL MIRANDA

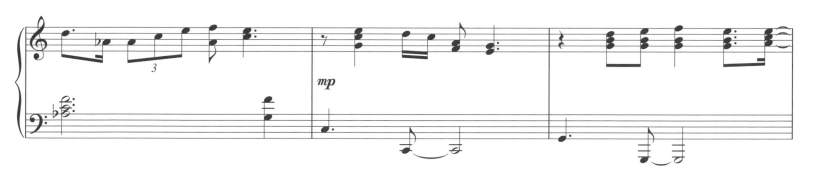

THE FAMILY MADRIGAL

Music and Lyrics by
LIN-MANUEL MIRANDA

Moderately fast

WAITING ON A MIRACLE

Music and Lyrics by
LIN-MANUEL MIRANDA

Moderately slow, in 2

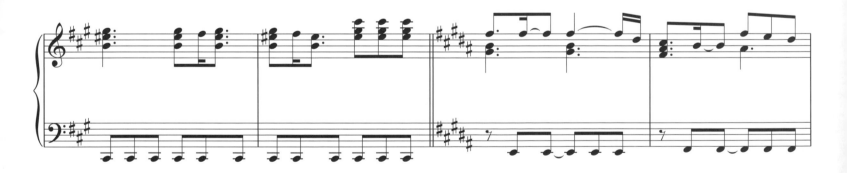

WE DON'T TALK ABOUT BRUNO

Music and Lyrics by
LIN-MANUEL MIRANDA

Moderately

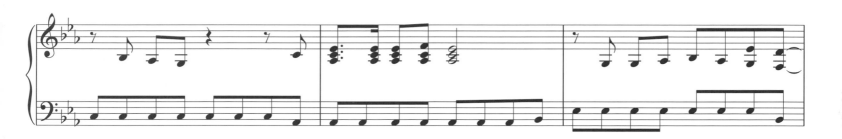

WHAT ELSE CAN I DO?

Music and Lyrics by
LIN-MANUEL MIRANDA

Play Your Favorite Disney Songs

Piano/Vocal/Guitar

00312480	Aladdin	$19.99
00359047	Alice in Wonderland	$19.99
00313000	And the Winner Is – 2nd Ed.	$17.99
00313055	The Aristocats	$19.99
00234049	Beauty and the Beast (2017)	$22.99
00311532	Beauty and the Beast Selections from the Movie	$17.99
00359192	The Best of Disney	$17.99
00103145	Brave	$19.99
00313499	Camp Rock 2 – The Final Jam	$16.99
00242528	Cars 3	$14.99
00359478	Cinderella	$17.99
00146069	Cinderella (2015)	$22.99
00253985	Coco	$19.99
00195620	Contemporary Disney – 3rd Edition	$29.99
00151969	Descendants	$22.99
00237613	Descendants 2	$19.99
00311523	The Disney Collection	$24.99
00283395	Disney Love Songs - 3rd Edition	$16.99
00313205	The Disney Theme Park Songbook	$27.99
00313588	Disney's Fairy Tale Weddings	$16.99
00313184	Disney's Princess Collection – Complete	$19.99
00248638	Disney Villains	$24.99
00398900	Encanto	$19.99
00124307	Frozen	$19.99
00313073	Hercules	$19.99
00313329	High School Musical	$19.99
00313045	The Hunchback of Notre Dame	$24.99
00256650	The Illustrated Treasury of Disney Songs – 7th Ed.	$34.99
00360154	Walt Disney's The Jungle Book	$19.99
00156370	The Lion Guard	$16.99
00312504	The Lion King	$19.99
00313624	The Lion King – Deluxe Edition	$19.99
00490238	The Little Mermaid	$19.99
00360439	Mary Poppins	$17.99
00204662	Moana	$19.99
00313099	Mulan	$19.99
00127534	The Muppets Most Wanted	$16.99
00311572	Newsies	$24.99
00315560	Newsies – Broadway Musical	$24.99
00253989	Olaf's Frozen Adventure	$16.99
00360819	Peter Pan	$17.99
00313013	Pocahontas	$19.99
00313482	The Princess and the Frog	$22.99
00125526	Saving Mr. Banks	$14.99
00362321	Soul	$19.99
00311525	A Souvenir Disney Songbook	$27.99
00313524	Tangled	$19.99
00313122	Tarzan	$22.99
00122118	Teen Beach Movie	$16.99
00313033	Toy Story	$19.99

Easy Piano

00222555	Aladdin	$17.99
00110003	Beauty and the Beast	$16.95
00234050	Beauty and the Beast (2017)	$17.99
00316039	Disney's Beauty and the Beast: The Broadway Musical	$17.99
00248749	Cars	$12.99
00285558	Christopher Robin	$17.99
00146948	Cinderella (2015)	$14.99
00254119	Coco	$17.99
00322831	Descendants	$19.99
00316040	Disney!	$24.99
00222535	The Disney Collection	$24.99
00193589	Disney Fun Songs	$17.99
00192459	Disney Greatest Love Songs	$17.99
00316075	Disney Hits	$14.99
00286966	Disney Latest Hits	$17.99
00316081	Disney Mega-Hit Movies – 2nd Ed.	$24.99
00310322	Disney's My First Songbook	$19.99
00316085	Disney's My First Songbook – Vol. 2	$17.99
00316123	Disney's My First Songbook – Vol. 3	$17.99
00316160	Disney's My First Songbook – Vol. 4	$17.99
00140978	Disney's My First Songbook – Vol. 5	$14.99
00313057	Disney's Princess Collection – Vol. 1	$16.99
00316034	Disney's Princess Collection – Vol. 2	$15.99
00399538	Encanto	$19.99
00316121	Enchanted	$12.95
00490553	Fantasia	$14.99
00194350	Finding Dory	$14.99
00274938	First 50 Disney Songs You Should Play on the Piano	$22.99
00125506	Frozen	$19.99
00279514	Frozen – The Broadway Musical	$19.99
00328775	Frozen 2	$19.99
00142790	Into the Woods	$19.99
00254118	Olaf's Frozen Adventure	$14.99
00316047	Walt Disney's The Jungle Book	$16.99
00316122	The Lion King – Broadway Selections	$19.99
00110029	The Lion King	$19.99
00490386	The Little Mermaid	$19.99
00316018	Mary Poppins	$15.99
00204664	Moana	$19.99
00119440	Newsies – Broadway Musical	$19.99
00316096	Pirates of the Caribbean – The Curse of the Black Pearl	$19.99
00311916	Really Easy Piano – Disney	$14.99
00302335	Toy Story Easy Piano Collection	$16.99
00129727	Up	$19.99
00277257	A Wrinkle in Time	$17.99
00276975	Zombies	$17.99

Piano Solo

00242909	Beauty and the Beast (2017)	$19.99
00192070	The BFG	$17.99
00285000	Christopher Robin	$17.99
00313131	Disney at the Piano	$15.99
00313150	Disney Classics	$12.95
00128219	Disney Hits for Piano Solo	$16.99
00242588	Disney Medleys for Piano Solo	$17.99
00313128	Disney Piano Solos	$17.99
00311754	Disney Songs for Classical Piano	$17.99
00194289	Finding Dory	$16.99
00128220	Frozen	$16.99
00154672	The Good Dinosaur	$16.99
00313290	The Incredibles	$16.99
00282473	Incredibles 2	$17.99
00148723	Inside Out	$22.99
00292060	The Lion King	$16.99
00131318	Maleficent	$14.99
00122213	The Monsters Collection	$16.99
00242537	Pirates of the Caribbean – Dead Men Tell No Tales	$16.99
00313579	Pirates of the Caribbean – On Stranger Tides	$16.99
00313380	Pirates of the Caribbean – At World's End	$19.99
00313343	Pirates of the Caribbean – Dead Man's Chest	$19.99
00313256	Pirates of the Caribbean – The Curse of the Black Pearl	$19.99
00362321	Soul	$19.99
00148720	Tomorrowland	$14.99
00313471	Up	$19.99

Piano/Vocal

00126656	Aladdin – Broadway Musical	$24.99
00312511	Disney's Beauty and the Beast: The Broadway Musical	$22.99
00230066	Disney Collected Kids' Solos	$36.99
00740197	Disney Solos for Kids	$19.99
00281007	Frozen – The Broadway Musical	$19.99
00313097	The Lion King – Broadway Selections	$19.99
00313402	The Little Mermaid	$24.99
00313303	Mary Poppins	$17.99
00740294	More Disney Solos for Kids	$19.99
00230032	Still More Disney Solos for Kids	$19.99

Fake Books

00275405	The Easy Disney Fake Book	$24.99
00175311	The Disney Fake Book – 4th Edition	$39.99

HAL•LEONARD®

Disney Characters and Artwork TM & © 2018 Disney

Prices, contents, and availability subject to change without notice.
Prices listed in U.S. dollars.